WITHDRAWN

MAKING LOVE

The Chapman Guide to
Making Sex an Act of Love

GARY D. CHAPMAN, PH.D.

TYNDALE HOUSE PUBLISHERS, INC.

Carol Stream, Illinois

Visit Tyndale's exciting Web site at www.tyndale.com

TYNDALE and Tyndale's quill logo are registered trademarks of Tyndale House Publishers, Inc.

Making Love: The Chapman Guide to Making Sex an Act of Love

Copyright © 2008 by Gary D. Chapman. All rights reserved.

Cover background image copyright © by Lanica Klein/iStockphoto. All rights reserved.

Cover photo by Ron Kaufmann. Copyright © 2007 by Tyndale House Publishers, Inc. All rights reserved.

Author photo copyright © by Boyce Shore & Associates. All rights reserved.

Designed by Ron Kaufmann

Edited by Kathryn S. Olson

All Scripture quotations, unless otherwise indicated, are taken from the Holy Bible, New International Version®. NIV®. Copyright © 1973, 1978, 1984 by International Bible Society. Used by permission of Zondervan. All rights reserved.

Scripture quotations marked NLT are taken from the *Holy Bible,* New Living Translation, copyright © 1996, 2004. Used by permission of Tyndale House Publishers, Inc., Carol Stream, Illinois 60188. All rights reserved.

Scripture quotations marked NKJV are taken from the New King James Version®. Copyright © 1982 by Thomas Nelson, Inc. Used by permission. All rights reserved. *NKJV* is a trademark of Thomas Nelson, Inc.

Library of Congress Cataloging-in-Publication Data

Chapman, Gary D., date.
    Making love : the Chapman guide to making sex an act of love / Gary D. Chapman.
        p. cm.
    Includes bibliographical references.
    ISBN-13: 978-1-4143-0018-4 (hc : alk. paper)
    ISBN-10: 1-4143-0018-2 (hc : alk. paper) 1. Sex—Religious aspects—Christianity. I. Title.
    BT708.C43 2008
    241'.66—dc22   2007033327

Printed in the United States of America

14   13   12   11   10   09   08
7   6   5   4   3   2   1

TABLE OF CONTENTS

Introduction

"*L*et's make love."

"Let's have sex."

Is there a difference? Most definitely. In fact, the two are worlds apart.

Sex is the joining of two bodies; love is the joining of two souls. When sex grows out of love, it becomes a deeply emotional, bonding experience. When having sex is viewed as nothing more than satisfying biological urges, that's all it does. It is never ultimately fulfilling. It is more animal than human.

Throughout human history, love and sex have always been related. However, in contemporary culture, love and sex have been equated. The common perception today is that *making love* means "having sex." Love is defined as a romantic feeling, and sex is its logical expression. Sex outside of marriage has become as common as sex within marriage. Sex has been separated from commitment and is viewed as a form of casual entertainment, much like being on a roller coaster or some other amusement-park ride. When it's over, we look forward to the next ride. This view of sex has left thousands feeling emotionally empty and longing for something to fill the void of the soul.

I believe that the Christian faith, which is built upon the Jewish faith, offers a wealth of insight on making love, not just having sex.

For example, both the Jewish faith and the Christian faith view sex as a gift from God. Both teach that God has given us guidelines on how to relate to each other sexually. It's interesting that recent sociological research has come to the same conclusions as those found in the ancient Jewish and Christian Scriptures. One such conclusion is that sex within marriage is much more meaningful and satisfying than sex outside of marriage.[1] While this truth is not popular in secular society, it bears the support of both research and Scripture.

The purpose of this book is to explore the Judeo-Christian teachings on love and sex and on how love and sex relate to each other. I believe sex without love will never be ultimately fulfilling, but sex that grows out of love will take a marriage to a whole new level of satisfaction. I feel certain that thousands of marriages can be greatly enhanced as couples learn to make love, not just have sex.

This book is not designed to be a comprehensive sex manual. My goal is to show you the difference between making love and simply having sex. Ideally, you and your spouse will read the book together, answer the questions at the end of each chapter, and then share your answers with each other. If you choose to do so, I believe you will find yourselves on the way to becoming real lovers.

However, if your spouse is not willing to read and discuss the book with you, it will still be well worth your time to read it yourself. I strongly urge you to follow the suggestions made in the book. Reach out to your spouse. Extend the opportunity for your husband or wife to respond to your efforts to stimulate growth in your relationship. I'm sure you know that you cannot force your spouse to do anything, but you can greatly influence your spouse by means of a loving attitude expressed in loving words and actions.

I have intentionally kept this book brief because I know you are busy. You can probably read it in less than two hours. You will find that reading this book will be a good investment of your time. At the end of each short chapter, you will find practical suggestions on how to weave these ideas into the fabric of your own marriage.

If you desire greater sexual satisfaction, you must learn to love.

1

*C*ontrary to popular belief, Hollywood did not invent sex. According to the most ancient Jewish writings, the Book of Beginnings, God looked at the man he had created and said, "It is not good for the man to be alone. I will make a helper suitable for him." The Creation narrative continues, "God caused the man to fall into a deep sleep; and while he was sleeping, he took one of the man's ribs and closed up the place with flesh. Then the LORD God made a woman from the rib he had taken out of the man, and he brought her to the man." The man exclaimed, "This is now bone of my bones and flesh of my flesh; she shall be called 'woman,' for she was taken out of man." Then the Creator declared that the two would "become one flesh." The account concludes with these words: "The man and his wife were both naked, and they felt no shame."[1]

SEX IS BEAUTIFUL

Based on this ancient Creation account, Jews and Christians have always viewed marriage as a sacred relationship between a husband and wife, instituted by God. The sexual union between the husband and wife is seen as a living symbol of their deep companionship. That Adam and Eve were naked and unashamed indicates that from God's perspective, sex is beautiful.

Throughout the Old and New Testament Scriptures, God repeatedly affirms the beauty of sexual intercourse within the marital relationship. While the Bible records incidents of polygamy, fornication (sex outside of marriage), adultery, homosexuality, incest, and rape, these distortions of sexuality are never approved by God. Sexual intercourse from God's perspective is an act of love that binds the souls of a husband and a wife to each other in a lifelong, intimate relationship.

THE PURPOSE OF SEX

It is obvious that one of the purposes of relating to each other sexually in the context of marriage is for reproduction. God himself said to Adam and Eve, "Be fruitful and increase in number; fill the earth and subdue it."[2] Husbands and wives who love each other and express their love sexually provide the healthiest context in which to rear children. It is interesting that contemporary research supports this ancient biblical pattern.[3]

However, procreation is not the only purpose, nor the primary purpose, of sexual intercourse within marriage. Far more basic are the psychological and spiritual dimensions of making love. As a husband and wife give themselves to each other sexually, they are building a psychological and spiritual bond that unites their souls at the deepest possible level. Together they can face the challenges of life because they are soul partners. Nothing unites a husband and wife more deeply than making love.

On the other hand, if the married couple is simply having sex without love, this bonding does not take place. Thus, the couple becomes estranged, and their union will eventually dissipate. For some, divorce is the culmination of this estrangement. Having sex without love builds resentment and, later, hostility.

God intends marital sex to be an experience of extreme pleasure. This pleasure is not limited to the physical sensation of orgasm. It also involves the emotions, the intellect, and the spirit. Sexual intercourse within marriage is designed to give us a taste of the divine. It involves the total person and brings waves of pleasure as we make love.

AN ANCIENT EXAMPLE

The books of Hebrew poetry found in the Old Testament seek to capture this pleasure. Here are the words of a husband speaking to his bride: "You have stolen my heart, my sister, my bride; you have stolen my heart with one glance of your eyes, with one jewel of your necklace. How delightful is your love, my sister, my bride! How much more pleasing is your love than wine, and the fragrance of your perfume than any spice! Your lips drop sweetness as the honeycomb, my bride; milk and

honey are under your tongue. The fragrance of your garments is like that of Lebanon. . . . You are a garden fountain, a well of flowing water streaming down from Lebanon." His bride responds, "Let my lover come into his garden and taste its choice fruits."[4]

A short time later, the wife says of her husband, "My lover is radiant and ruddy, outstanding among ten thousand. His head is purest gold; his hair is wavy and black as a raven. . . . His cheeks are like beds of spice. . . . His arms are rods of gold. . . . His legs are pillars of marble. . . . His mouth is sweetness itself; he is altogether lovely. This is my lover, this my friend."[5]

Obviously, these ancient lovers are finding great pleasure in relating to each other sexually. They are discovering what it means to make love, not just have sex.

ACCENTUATE THE POSITIVE

Notice particularly in the passages above that the husband and the wife each accentuated the positive characteristics of the other.

Contemporary couples, in contrast, often tend to focus on the negative. Even though there were many, many positive characteristics that drew them to each other when they first met, when conflicts begin to emerge, they focus on the negative. They verbalize these by saying such things as, "I can't believe you are so lazy." "I have never known anyone as selfish as you." "You are just like your father. No wonder your mother left him." Such statements create hurt, anger, and resentment. And typically an offended spouse reciprocates with more negative statements. When we focus on the negative, we draw out the worst in our spouse.

On the other hand, when we choose to focus on the positive, we stimulate a positive response. The wife who says, "Wow. Do you ever look tough tonight!" will likely receive not only a smile but also positive words about the way she looks. The spouse who says, "Thanks for cooking the meal; it was delicious," stimulates warm, positive feelings in the heart of the one who prepared the meal. When we focus on the positive and verbalize our appreciation and admiration for each other, we create a climate in which sex can become a genuine expression of love.

Sex was designed by God to be a mutually satisfying experience whereby husbands and wives express their love, intimacy, and commitment to each other. A husband and wife may engage in sexual intercourse without feelings of love, intimacy, and commitment, but this has never been God's ideal. God's intention is for couples to make love, not just have sex.

PUTTING THE PRINCIPLES INTO PRACTICE

1. How would you explain the difference between making love and just having sex?

2. On a scale of 1–10, with 10 being the highest, how would you rank your success at "making love"? How do you think your spouse would rank you?

3. What would you like your spouse to do (or stop doing) that would make the sexual relationship more meaningful for you?

4. What could you do (or stop doing) to make the sexual relationship more meaningful for your spouse?

5. Would you be willing to share your answers to the above questions with your spouse?

2

*S*ex can be quick, but love requires time. I am not denying that a "quickie" can sometimes be an expression of love. What I am saying is that finding mutual sexual satisfaction in marriage takes time. I have always found it interesting that God instructed the young men and women of Israel to take a year for their honeymoon: "A newly married man must not be drafted into the army or be given any other official responsibilities. He must be free to spend one year at home, bringing happiness to the wife he has married."[1]

The reality is that not many couples find mutual sexual fulfillment in less than a year. Just as they must grow together intellectually, emotionally, and spiritually, they must also grow together sexually. It is a process that takes time. Making love is more than inserting the penis into the vagina and having an orgasm. Making love has as its object mutual pleasure in the process.

Why does it take so much time to grow together sexually? Because males and females are different in just about every way you could imagine—physically, emotionally, and psychologically. There are key differences between men and women in the nature of the sex drive, in the ignition points that make them ready for sex, and even in their responses during intercourse. A husband and wife must discover and accept these differences before they can begin to find mutual satisfaction.

NATURE OF THE SEX DRIVE

While both men and women have a biological drive to have sex, the female's drive or desire is far more tied to her emotions than is the man's. If a woman feels loved by her husband, she desires to be sexually intimate with him. However, if she does not feel loved, she may have little desire to have sex with him. (An exception might be the case in which sex is the only way she gets tender touch and kind words that speak to her emotionally.) This difference explains a lot of things for us. For example, it explains how a husband and wife can have an intense argument and say hateful things to each other, but thirty minutes later the husband wants to have intercourse. The wife will find that virtually impossible unless he apologizes in a way that she considers sincere. Then, perhaps, her sexual desire can be kindled.

A husband can desire to have sexual intercourse even when things are not right in the relationship. In fact, he often thinks that having sex will solve the problems. For the male, when the seminal vesicles are full and the testosterone level is normal, there will be a desire for sexual release. This desire is not deeply rooted in his emotions but rather in his biological urges. On the other hand, a wife wants things to be made right before having sexual intercourse. Sex itself does not solve problems for her.

Understanding this difference in the nature of sexual desire will help a husband give far more attention to his wife's emotional needs, which we will discuss further in chapters 4 and 5. It will also help a wife understand why her husband's desire for sexual intimacy can be just as strong after a fight as it was before the fight.

This difference also explains why couples often disagree on the frequency of sexual intercourse. A husband's desire is guided largely by the buildup of seminal fluid, which creates a physiological need for release. This is methodical and regular and has little to do with how things are going in a couple's relationship. While the wife's biological clock is influenced to some degree by her monthly menstrual cycle, her physiological urges are often overridden by her emotions and the quality of the relationship. Couples must learn to work with this difference in the nature of sexual desire if they are to find mutual fulfillment.

IGNITION POINTS

Another difference is in the area of ignition points, or what each finds sexually stimulating. The male is strongly stimulated by sight; the female, by touch and kind words. This explains why a husband can merely watch his wife getting ready for bed, and by the time she gets undressed, he is ready to have intercourse. On the other hand, she can watch him undress without the thought of sex ever crossing her mind. However, if the husband speaks kind words and uses tender touch, assuming that their marital relationship is fairly positive, her sexual urges will be ignited. Understanding this difference and cooperating with it will help a couple get on the same page. If they ignore this difference, a husband and wife may never find mutual fulfillment.

Incidentally, this difference also explains why men are far more tempted by pornography than women are, and why women are more likely to become emotionally involved with a coworker who speaks kind words and uses tender touch. While it's helpful to recognize these gender-specific areas of temptation, please understand that I am not offering excuses for giving in to them. Let me be perfectly clear: To yield to either of these temptations is seriously detrimental to a marriage, as well as to spiritual health. There is no place for pornography in the life of a Christian husband, and it is equally unacceptable for a Christian wife to allow herself to become emotionally attached to another man. While working on our own sexual fulfillment, we must guard our hearts from falling into these destructive patterns.

RESPONSES

Another difference between men and women is in the context of sexual intercourse itself. The male's response tends to be fast and explosive, while the female's response tends to be slow and lasting. The male tends to reach climax quickly, and after climax, he's finished; it's all over for him—but the wife may be lying there thinking, *What's supposed to be so great about this?* She was only getting started. In order to find mutual sexual pleasure, both spouses need to understand this difference and learn to cooperate with each other. Research indicates that the average male will ejaculate after two minutes of vigorous thrusting.[2] The problem is that few women can reach orgasm in that short amount of time. Besides that, most women reach orgasm not through thrusting but through stimulation of the clitoris. This has led many couples to conclude that it is best for the wife to have orgasm as a part of the foreplay. Once she has experienced orgasm, then the husband is free to experience his own climax.

Many wives do not desire to have an orgasm every time they have intercourse. Sometimes, a wife is happy simply to experience tender touch, hear kind words, and sense her husband's love and closeness. He experiences climax and feels loved by her. They both find the experience to be satisfying even though she does not experience orgasm. A husband might object, saying, "I don't want to enjoy the sexual experience if she's not going to enjoy it." What he needs to realize is that she does enjoy making love, even if it doesn't always end in orgasm. It often requires far more energy, effort, and time for a woman to experience orgasm than it does for a man. Sometimes, because of fatigue or other distractions, a wife simply does not desire to go through the entire process. Her husband should not expect it of her. The goal is to pleasure each other. The wife should have the freedom to decide whether she desires to experience orgasm as a part of the whole sexual experience.

I have often been asked why God created men and women with all these sexual differences. I have said facetiously that if God had asked me, I would have suggested, "Don't even turn us on until we finish all our education. Then once you turn us on, let everyone get married three months later. After marriage, push both spouses' buttons every three days." Wouldn't that be a lot easier? I have concluded that God's intention, when he made us different, was for sex to be more than a reproductive act—that it would in fact be a chance to tangibly show our love. When sex is an act of love, the husband and wife approach each other and ask, "How may I pleasure you?" If we don't make it an act of love, we will never find mutual fulfillment.

If a husband and wife simply do "what comes naturally," they will never learn to make love. The best that may happen is that one of them will find partial fulfillment and the other will feel used. That is where thousands of couples are in their sexual relationship. They have sex from time to time, but they have never learned to make love. When we understand our differences, accept our differences, and learn how to work together, we can make beautiful music.

All of this takes time, patience, and understanding. If the two of you have never read and discussed a book on sexual technique, I would suggest Dr. Kevin Leman's book, *Sheet Music: Uncovering the Secrets of Sexual Intimacy in Marriage.*[3] With a little information and a lot of patience, the two of you can learn to make love.

PUTTING THE PRINCIPLES INTO PRACTICE

1. While both males and females have biological sexual drives, the female's sexual desire is greatly influenced by her emotions. Thus, if a wife does not feel loved, she may be reluctant

to engage sexually with her husband. How do you experience this reality in your marriage?

Husbands: Would you be willing to ask your wife to share with you the kinds of things you can do or say to best communicate your love to her?

Wives: Would you be willing to share with your husband what actions on his part tend to make you feel loved?

2. The male is strongly stimulated by sight; the female, by touch and kind words. How has this difference influenced your marriage?

Husbands: Would you be willing to ask your wife to share with you the kinds of touches and caring words that enhance her sexual desire?

Wives: Would you be willing to ask your husband to share with you the kinds of things you could do visually to stimulate him sexually?

3. The timing of orgasm is frustrating for many couples. The most common problem is the husband's ejaculating while the wife is still warming up to the sexual experience. He is finished and she is frustrated.

> Husbands: Would you be willing to discuss with your wife a solution that has worked for many couples: the husband bringing the wife to orgasm by stimulation of the clitoris as a part of the foreplay? Then once she has experienced orgasm, he is free to experience climax.

> Wives: Would you be willing to discuss with your husband your preferences related to orgasm?

3

LOVE GIVES BUT NEVER DEMANDS

$\mathcal{S}$ome Christians like to use the Scriptures as a club to demand their sexual rights in marriage. One Scripture passage often used is 1 Corinthians 7:3-5: "The husband should fulfill his marital duty to his wife, and likewise the wife to her husband. The wife's body does not belong to her alone but also to her husband. In the same way, the husband's body does not belong to him alone but also to his wife. Do not deprive each other." The husband reads this to his wife and demands that she perform her "wifely duties." Or a frustrated wife will say, "All I want is for him to be a husband to me. Is that asking too much?"

The apostle Paul sets out the marital ideal: A husband will reach out and seek to meet his wife's sexual needs, and she will do the same for him. That is a picture of true lovemaking. However, we are not to *demand* the ideal; instead, we are to *create* the ideal. Most of us find it easier to preach the ideal than to practice it.

So what is the process that brings us to the point of mutual lovemaking? I believe it begins with prayer. We each ask God to give us the attitude of Christ toward our spouse. A husband is specifically challenged to love his wife as Christ loved the church and gave himself up for her.[1] Christ loved the church before the church loved him; that is, he took the initiative. He loved the church in the face of rejection, and he loved the church all the way to death. There is no limit to his love. What is our response to such love? The Scriptures say, "We love [God] because he first loved us."[2] His love stimulated our love. God did not force us to do anything, but his love won our hearts.

This is the pattern for marriage. The husband takes the initiative to love his wife—and to persist in that love even through times of rejection. When the wife sees that he is unconditionally committed to her well-being, she respects him, and to use the language of Hebrew poetry, she invites him into her garden to enjoy the pleasures that she has ready for him.

Listen to the words of love that flow from the heart of a Hebrew husband from ancient times: "How beautiful you are, my darling! Oh, how beautiful! Your eyes . . . are doves. Your hair is like a flock of goats. . . . Your teeth are like a flock of sheep just shorn, coming up from the washing. Each has its twin; not one of them is alone. Your lips are like a scarlet ribbon; your mouth is lovely. Your temples behind your veil are like the halves of a pomegranate. Your neck is like the tower of David, built with elegance. . . . Your two breasts are like two fawns, like twin fawns of a gazelle that browse among the lilies. Until the day breaks and the shadows flee, I will go to the mountain of myrrh and to the hill of incense. All beautiful you are, my darling; there is no flaw in you."[3]

Husbands, if you want to speak words of love to your wife, you might use this as a model. Of course, you will need to update the metaphors. But I'm sure you're creative enough to do that.

What do these tender, affirming words do for a wife? They ignite her passion. She invites her husband to taste the sexual fruits of her body when she responds, "Awake, north wind, and come, south wind! Blow on my garden, that its fragrance may spread abroad. Let my lover come into his garden and taste its choice fruits."[4]

The husband responds to her invitation: "I have come into my garden, my sister, my bride; I have gathered my myrrh with my spice. I have eaten my honeycomb and my honey; I have drunk my wine and my milk."[5] Wow! That is making love, not just having sex.

The pattern is clear. The husband takes the initiative, not in demanding sex but in loving his wife. His words of affirmation describing her beauty touch her heart and make her want to be sexually intimate with him. Notice carefully that he did not enter the garden until she invited him. This is a part of lovemaking that many husbands do not understand. They are happy to take initiative—but in most husbands' minds, that means initiating a sexual encounter. The husband is sexually stimulated and assumes his wife has the same desire. So he barges ahead and enters the garden long before she is ready to invite him. The results? They end up having sex, but not making love.

Waiting for his wife's invitation can be frustrating for a man. One husband said, "I've been waiting for six months. How much longer do I wait?" The answer is not simply continuing to wait but rather giving love. The passage of time will not stimulate sexual arousal in a wife, but consistent love will.

I am fully aware that the pattern I have just presented is contrary to "what comes naturally." By nature, we tend to expect our spouse to meet our sexual needs. If our needs aren't met, then we start demanding. Such demands create resentment and drive our spouse further away. Making love is about giving, not demanding. When we focus on creating an atmosphere of love in which we are genuinely seeking to affirm our spouse, we will eventually hear the invitation.

All of this requires a change of heart. Each of us is by nature egocentric—thinking the world revolves around "me." Christ was not self-centered. He focused on his mission of loving the church and giving himself for it. When we ask God to change our perspective, then allow him to do so, we are on the road to making love, not just having sex.

PUTTING THE PRINCIPLES INTO PRACTICE

1. Has your attitude about sex leaned more toward giving or toward demanding?

2. Would you be willing to ask God to give you the attitude of Christ toward your spouse— taking the initiative to give rather than waiting and expecting to receive?

3. Think about ways in which your words or actions may be creating frustration or resent-

ment in your spouse. What can you say or do differently in the future?

4. Ask God to change your perspective—and then allow him to do it.

4

A wife is sitting in my office saying, "I just feel like my husband doesn't love me. He treats me like trash and then wants me to have sex with him. I don't understand that. I can't have sex with a man who doesn't love me." This wife knows deep within her heart that sex and love are supposed to go together. Sex without love seems like rape, and she cannot bear that. Many wives can identify with her pain.

On the other hand, many husbands experience the same frustration. I shall never forget the husband who said, "We had sex, but I felt like

I was with a corpse." Sex without love is indeed dead.

The desire for love is universal. When we are married, the love we most long for is that of our spouse. When we feel loved, the world looks bright. Sex is the cherry on top of the sundae. All of life is sweet. Without love, the world looks bleak, and sex is at best a temporary oasis in a barren desert.

Most couples do not know how to create love when it is absent. Many feel hopeless. "We've lost our feelings for each other; maybe we shouldn't have married" is a common sentiment. The tendency is for couples to blame marriage for the loss of their euphoric feelings. In reality, they would have lost those feelings even if they had not married.

TWO STAGES OF LOVE

The average lifespan of the "in love" experience is two years. We don't stay obsessed with each other forever. If we did, we would never accomplish anything. One man who was passionately in love told me, "I'm afraid I'm going to lose my job. Since

I met Julie, I can't focus my attention at work." It's hard to focus on anything else when we are in love. All our energy and all our thoughts focus on being with each other. When we are together, we are supremely happy; when we are apart, we long to be together.

What many fail to realize is that there are two distinct stages of romantic or emotional love. The first stage is the super-emotional high of the "in love" obsession. In this stage, we are pushed along by our emotions. Our acts of kindness require little effort. We would gladly climb the highest mountain or swim the deepest sea for each other. Without a second thought, we buy gifts we cannot afford and make promises we can never keep. It's great fun! But it is temporary. It cannot be sustained over a long period of time.

The second stage of love is far more realistic and requires thought and effort. We are no longer caught up in the waves of strong emotion. We have lost the illusion that the other person is perfect. We have returned to the real world of preparing meals, washing dishes, cleaning bathrooms, and perhaps changing a baby's diaper. Our differences have emerged; we find ourselves in conflict over minute issues. Our emotions have plummeted and turned sour. If we let our emotions take the lead, we will begin to argue with each other. Arguments lead to resentment, and resentment destroys our intimacy. Stage 1 has come to an end, but no one has told us how to enter stage 2.

THE CHALLENGES OF STAGE 2

The reason stage 2 is difficult is that it doesn't begin with exciting, exhilarating emotions but rather with a conscious choice. Stage 1 begins with the tingles; stage 2 begins with choosing a positive attitude.

One husband told me of his journey: "In the early days of our marriage, we struggled greatly. I found myself with negative feelings toward my wife. She did not live up to my expectations, and I'm sure she would have said the same about me. I finally decided that I did not marry a perfect woman, and she did not marry a perfect man. It's true—we had our differences, but I didn't marry her to make her miserable. I wanted us to learn to work together as a team and enjoy life together and rear our children in a loving home. So I decided I would ask God to help me learn how to be a good husband. The next Sunday, our pastor spoke about husbands and read the verse that says we are supposed to love our wives as Christ loved the church. I figured God was answering my prayer. So I asked God to show me how to love my wife. The first thought that came to my mind was *Why don't you ask her?* So I did.

"That afternoon I said to her, 'I want to become the best husband in the world, and I'm asking you to teach me how. Once a week I want you to tell me one thing that would make me a better husband, and I will work on it.' She was eager to help me," he said with a smile. "Within two months, she asked me to give her ideas on how to be a better wife. That was fifteen years ago. Now we have a great marriage. Both of us are happy, and our children are wonderful."

"What about the sexual aspect of your marriage?" I asked. He looked at me with a twinkle in his eye and said, "It couldn't be better." I knew they were making love, not just having sex.

IT ALL BEGINS WITH ATTITUDE

That husband's journey illustrates the principle that the second stage of love begins with an attitude. The attitude expresses itself in acts of kindness that, in turn, stimulate warm feelings. Those couples who learn to move from stage 1 to stage 2 of emotional love are the couples who learn how to make love, not just have sex.

Too many couples simply wait, hoping that "the tingles" will return. When they don't, their attitude and behavior become negative, and they destroy what they most want—a happy marriage. Emotional love can be restored, but it doesn't happen simply with the passing of time. It comes only when couples choose the attitude of love and find meaningful ways to express it. Loving actions stimulate loving feelings.

Sexual fulfillment has little to do with technique but much to do with attitude, words, and actions. The underlying questions are, Am I expressing love to my spouse? Is my attitude characterized by love? Am I truly looking out for my spouse's interests? Is my major concern to meet his or her needs? If these are my sincere desires, then I must examine my words and my actions. Am I communicating to my spouse by the way I talk and by what I say that I am committed to his or her well-being? Do I view my spouse as a gift from God and see myself as God's agent for building him or her up to become everything he desires? Do my actions reflect my love? When I cook a meal, do I do it as an expression of love to my spouse or do I do it with resentment? When I carry out the garbage, do I do it with an attitude of love or do I complain as I do it? When my words and actions reflect the love of Christ, I am on the road to having a sexual relationship that not only brings satisfaction to the two of us but brings pleasure to God. Making life better for my spouse is the theme of love.

We choose our attitude daily. When we choose to be negative, critical, condemning, and demanding, we stimulate negative feelings in the heart of our spouse. On the other hand, when we choose to be positive, affirming, encouraging, and giving, we stimulate positive emotions.

I am convinced that the most powerful prayer you can pray for your marriage is, "Lord, give me the attitude of Christ toward my spouse." Pray that prayer daily. It is a prayer that God will answer. The theme of Christ's life was one of service to others. When that attitude permeates your behavior toward your spouse, you will be on the way to making love. The way you treat each other through the day determines whether you will make love or simply have sex. Sex without love will never give you a satisfying marriage.

A good way to express an attitude of service to your spouse is to ask what you can do to make his or her life easier, or what you can do to be a better husband or wife. Listen carefully to the suggestions offered, and you will begin to learn how to express your love in ways that are especially meaningful to your spouse.

When each of you feels genuinely loved, appreciated, and respected by the other, it brings a

whole new level of love to your sexual relationship.
The rewards are priceless.

PUTTING THE PRINCIPLES
INTO PRACTICE

1. Which of the following best describes your
   marital relationship?

   ___ We are definitely still experiencing the
   "in love" stage.

   ___ We have made the transition and are in
   stage 2 of romantic love.

   ___ We are caught in the middle, definitely
   out of stage 1 but not yet into stage 2.

2. If you are caught in the middle, how would
   you describe your present attitude?

3. Would you be willing to ask God to give you
   the attitude of Christ toward your spouse—
   an attitude of service and love?

4. Would you be willing to admit to your
   spouse that you have had a negative attitude
   and that you have asked God to teach you

how to be the husband or wife that your
spouse deserves?

5. Ask your spouse, "Will you give me one idea
every week about how I could be a better
spouse to you? I'm willing to work on it if
you will tell me what you would like."

5

*A*s you have been reading this book, perhaps you have thought, *I've tried some of these things, but they didn't seem to make a difference. No matter what I do, it doesn't seem to be enough to satisfy my spouse.* Throughout my counseling career I have encountered hundreds of couples who are sincerely trying to express love to each other and to make the sexual part of the marriage a genuine act of love. But they have been frustrated because their expressions of love haven't seemed to be "enough" for their spouses.

I remember Marc, who said, "I really wanted to do something special for Jill. I wanted her to know how much I loved her, so I spent a lot of money on a ring that I thought she would like. I planned to give her the ring at the end of a romantic evening. We had dinner together at a very nice restaurant and took a walk in a botanical garden. I told her I had a surprise for her and that I wanted her to know how much I loved her. Then I gave her the ring. She was very appreciative and gave me a big kiss and hug. I anticipated that later that evening we would have a dynamite sexual experience, but she said, 'I'm too tired.' I spent the next two hours lying in bed beside my wife wondering, *What does a man have to do to get a little love from his wife?*"

Marc genuinely desired to make sex with his wife an act of love. He thought that a romantic dinner, followed by a walk in a beautiful garden, topped off with an expensive gift would surely create the climate for a loving sexual experience. The problem was not his sincerity; he was extremely sincere. The problem was his mistaken concept of what would make his wife *feel* loved. His idea was that any woman would feel loved if a man did what he had done that evening. What he did not take into account is that people have different love languages. What makes one woman feel loved will not necessarily make another woman feel loved.

In my counseling with Marc and Jill, I found that Jill's primary love language was *acts of service.* What really made her feel loved was having Marc help her with household projects, doing something to "lighten her load." Marc was speaking the language of *quality time,* giving his wife an evening of undivided attention, and the love language of *gifts.* While both of these were appreciated by Jill, they did not deeply touch her heart as sincere expressions of love. She had been asking him for months to help her with the dishes, take out the trash, vacuum the floors, and wash her car. Her requests had fallen on deaf ears.

In Marc's mind, household chores were not the responsibility of the husband, and why should he wash her car when he didn't even wash his own? It cost only three dollars to drive it through a car wash. She could do that as well as he could. But the result was that Jill didn't feel loved by Marc; rather, she was beginning to resent him. Dinner at a nice restaurant, a walk in the garden, and a nice gift did not compensate for the hurt and sense of rejection that she felt. He was sincere, but he was not expressing his love in the most effective language.

THE FIVE LOVE LANGUAGES

After counseling hundreds of couples, I have discovered that there are five fundamental ways to express love. I call them the five love languages. Several years ago I wrote a book with that title. It has now sold over four million copies and has been translated into thirty-five languages around the world.[1] In this chapter, I want to give you a brief summary of these languages.

Each of us has a primary love language; that is, one of the five languages speaks more deeply to us than the other four. It is very similar to spoken language. All of us grew up speaking a language with a dialect (I grew up speaking English Southern style). It is this language and dialect that we understand best. The same is true with emotional love. If your spouse speaks your primary love language, you will feel loved and appreciated. If your spouse does not speak your love language, you may feel unloved even though your spouse is speaking some of the other love languages.

I have already alluded to most of these languages, but let me state them clearly and tell you a little about each one.

WORDS OF AFFIRMATION

The Scriptures say "Love edifies."[2] That is, love builds up another person. When you speak the language of words of affirmation, you are using words to express love and appreciation to your spouse.

- "Wow! Do you ever look nice in that outfit."

- "Thanks for taking the recycling out."

- "Great meal! I really appreciate all your hard work."

- ∾ "I felt really proud of you when I saw you reading a Bible story to Jennifer tonight."

- ∾ "Thanks for putting gas in my car. That was a real help."

- ∾ "Your hair looks very nice."

- ∾ "I'm glad you volunteered to teach the five-year-olds in Sunday school. You'll do a great job. Children love you."

- ∾ "You're losing weight and looking nice. Of course, I would love you even if you didn't lose weight."

All these statements are words of affirmation. Words of affirmation may focus on your spouse's personality: "I love the fact that you're so organized. It saves us so much time." Or, "Your optimism encourages me to always try." Words of affirmation may also focus on some accomplishment your spouse has made: "I'm so pleased that you are taking that course on computers. I knew you could do it." "I was so proud of you when you caught that long fly ball in the softball game tonight. That play won the game for your team." This love language may also focus on your spouse's physical appearance: "I feel so secure when I touch the muscles in your arm." "I love your blue eyes. They are always so sparkling."

Nothing makes a person whose primary love language is words of affirmation feel more loved than the positive words you speak. Conversely, if you speak harsh, negative words, your spouse will be extremely hurt and will not quickly recover. It will be almost impossible for your spouse to make love after hearing harsh words from you. If this is your spouse's primary love language, you must learn to speak it fluently if you want to make sex an act of love.

RECEIVING GIFTS

For some people, nothing speaks more deeply of love than a thoughtful gift. The gift communicates that someone was thinking of them. The gift may be as simple as a wildflower picked out of the yard or as expensive as the ring that Marc gave Jill. The important thing is not how much the gift cost but that someone was thinking about them. The gift is a visible indication of thoughtfulness and communicates love loudly.

If receiving gifts is your spouse's primary love language, you will need to learn to give gifts regularly. You do not need to be a millionaire to speak this language. Some gifts are free: a four-leaf clover, a coin you found in the parking lot, a "treasure" that you have saved from your childhood, a "prize" found in a cereal box. Other gifts are very inexpensive: a candy bar, an ice-cream cone, a single rose purchased from a street vendor, your spouse's favorite magazine, or a charm for her bracelet. Other gifts are much more expensive, such as tickets to a professional sports event, diamonds and rubies, membership at the local gym, or a pampering treatment at a local spa. Your spouse knows what your budget can afford. The person whose love language is gifts doesn't expect gifts that are financially unreasonable. But such a spouse does expect evidence of your love, and that means gifts.

Perhaps receiving gifts is not very meaningful to you. If so, you have probably been reluctant to give gifts to your spouse. However, if receiving gifts is your spouse's primary love language, then you have been missing out on the most effective way to express your love. It will take time to learn to "speak" this language. You may need to engage the help of your wife's sister or your husband's brother for ideas. Or you may ask your spouse to make a list of the kinds of gifts that would be meaningful.

If receiving gifts is your spouse's primary love language, then don't let a single special day pass without giving a special gift. Then sprinkle in gifts on nonspecial days too.

ACTS OF SERVICE

The third love language is *acts of service*—doing things for your spouse that you know your spouse would like you to do. If you have been married for a few years, you probably know what they are because your spouse has requested them through the years:

- "Will you give the baby a bath while I finish the dishes?"

- "Would you take the trash out tonight, please?"

ᵔ "Would you mind driving my car to pick up Stephanie? Also, it would be helpful if you would stop on the way home and get some gas and wash my windshield."

ᵔ "Would you stop by the pharmacy and pick up my prescription?"

ᵔ "Would it be possible for you to mow the grass on Friday evening? My sister is coming over on Saturday."

ᵔ "Could you make a cherry cobbler this week? I love your cherry cobblers."

All these questions are requests for acts of service. If your spouse has requested something once, you can assume it is something that would be appreciated on a regular basis.

If acts of service is your spouse's primary love language, then your positive response to a request communicates your love in a powerful way. On the other hand, when you ignore a request, your spouse will feel unloved. An expensive gift will not take the place of your regularly taking out the recycling. This is the discovery that Marc made when he and Jill were in counseling.

Speaking the love language of your spouse enhances the sexual relationship because your spouse now feels loved. I remember the husband who said to me, "I wish someone had told me twenty years ago that my taking out the garbage was sexy for my wife. For me, it was just another responsibility. Had I known it was sexy, I would have taken out the garbage twice a day!" He learned a little late, but at least he learned.

QUALITY TIME

Quality time means giving your spouse your undivided attention. If this is your spouse's primary love language, nothing is more important than the two of you having uninterrupted time together.

Some people think of quality time as simply two people being together. I remember the husband who said to me, "I knew she liked football as much as I did, so I got tickets to the game. She had told me that quality time was her love language. I expected that after a whole evening together, she would really feel loved. I was shocked when we got home that night and she said to me, 'Alex, do you really love me?'

"I said, 'You know I love you. That's why I got tickets to the game. You told me that quality time was your love language and I wanted us to have some time together.' She shook her head, walked off, and started crying.

"That's when I knew I was missing something. Later she said, 'We were together; that's true, but we were not focusing on each other. Our attention was on the game. You talked to the man beside you and the man in front of you, but you said almost nothing to me. On the way home, all we talked about was the game. We were together for four hours, but you never asked me anything about myself. Sometimes I wonder if you really care.'

"I assured her that I did care about her and that I loved her very much, but I could tell that my words sounded empty to her. That's the night I picked up the book *The Five Love Languages* and started reading it. She had been asking me for months to read it. She had told me about the concept and that her language was quality time. But I knew I was missing it.

"As I read the book, I realized that what she wanted was my undivided attention. She wanted me to sit on the couch with her, to take a walk with her, or to ask her questions and express interest in what was going on in her life. She didn't want to compete with the television or the computer. She wanted to know that she was number one in my life. I realized that my efforts to speak her language had missed the mark."

He continued, "The next day I took the book to work and finished reading it. That night I told her that I had read it and realized that I had failed to understand what she meant by quality time. I told her how sorry I was and that I wanted her to know how much I loved her. I asked her if she would like for us to initiate a 'daily sharing time' in which we would take twenty to thirty minutes every evening, sit down with the TV off, and talk with each other about what was going on in our lives. She said, 'That's what I've been wanting for so long.'

"That was the beginning of a whole new chapter in our marriage. Some nights when she felt like it, we would take a walk together. Other nights we sat on the couch and talked. Within two weeks, I saw her whole attitude toward me begin to change. Things in the bedroom changed. I had begun to think that she had lost interest in sex, but now she was taking the initiative. It was hard for me to believe that a little 'talking time' every day could make such a difference in her attitude.

"My love language is words of affirmation," he said. "And she is now speaking my language. For several months before 'the change,' she had been giving me critical words almost every day. That was one of the reasons I tried to stay away from her. I not only felt unloved, I felt like she didn't even like me, that nothing I did was enough. If only I had focused my energy on speaking her love language, things would have been different years earlier. Now that we have the love part figured out, sex has never been better."

What Alex discovered is that quality time is not simply being in the same house or at the same ball game. It is, rather, giving undivided attention, expressing interest in what is going on in the other person's life. Going to the ball game can be an expression of quality time if you spend some of that time looking into your spouse's eyes, asking questions, expressing interest so that your spouse feels more important than the game. You must talk with him or her more than with the man next to you or in front of you.

The difference is focus. Is your focus on the game, or is your focus on your spouse? The latter is quality time; the former is simply going to a ball game. Quality time involves asking questions about your spouse's activities, desires, thoughts, and feelings—and listening to the answers.

One warning: If in such a quality-time conversation your spouse shares struggles and frustrations, don't jump quickly to offer answers. When you give quick fixes, your spouse senses that you don't understand the problem. A better approach is to affirm your spouse's feelings and frustrations by saying, "I can see how that would be very frustrating. I think that would frustrate me as well." Then ask, "Is there anything I could do that might be helpful?" Be responsive to any suggestions. If your spouse asks for your advice, give it; but offer it as "something that might help," not as the thing that will solve the problem. What your spouse is looking for is understanding and support. You don't need to play the role of a parent and give instructions on what to do.

If your spouse's love language is quality time, I would encourage you to establish a daily sharing time as quickly as possible (that is, if your spouse agrees that this would be something he or she would appreciate). You will be on the road to filling the emotional love tank of your spouse—and that full love tank will spill over into the bedroom.

PHYSICAL TOUCH

Physical touch is a powerful communicator. We will talk in the next chapter about negative physical touch: physical and sexual abuse. Here we're talking about positive, affirming touches. Holding hands, embracing, kissing, putting your arm around her shoulder, putting your hand on his neck are all affirming touches.

For some people, physical touch is the primary method of receiving love. If such a person does not receive affirming touches from a spouse, he or she will feel unloved even though the spouse may be giving words of affirmation, gifts, acts of service, and quality time. The reasoning is, "If you seldom touch me, it means you seldom think about me. I am unimportant in your life."

These people will normally be touchers themselves. This is the man who is reaching out to give a pat on the back to everyone he encounters. This is the woman who is hugging everyone she meets. They are touching others because in their minds this is the way to express love.

Perhaps you grew up in a nontouching family. Touching does not come naturally for you. Now you find yourself married to someone for whom physical touch is the primary love language. What are you to do? The answer is simple—learn to touch. The first few times you reach out to initiate affirming touch may seem awkward or unnatural to you. I assure you it will be meaningful to your spouse. The more you do it, the easier it becomes. Make it your goal to lovingly touch your spouse every day. If your spouse's love language is physical touch, a hug before you leave the house and a kiss when you return will do wonders in the bedroom.

Sexual intercourse obviously involves physical touch. However, if you touch your spouse only when you have sex, and your spouse's primary love language is physical touch, I can tell you sex will not be an act of love. One wife said, "The only time he ever touches me is when he wants to have intercourse. I never get a kiss, he never hugs me, he never takes my hand when we get out of the car. He never holds my hand when we sit together. My primary love language is physical touch. My emotional love tank is on empty. Then he wants to have sex. It's almost more than I can bear. I feel so unloved by him." This husband is having sex, but he is not making love.

Because of the biological male sex drive, some husbands will automatically jump to the conclusion that their primary love language is physical touch, which they equate with having sex. My questions to them are: Do nonsexual touches make you feel loved? When she gives you a hug or a kiss that does not lead to sexual intercourse, do you feel loved? Do you like her to hold your hand as you walk down the sidewalk? Do you enjoy her sitting close to you on the couch? If these nonsexual touches do not communicate emotional love, then your primary love language is not physical touch.

DISCOVERING YOUR SPOUSE'S LOVE LANGUAGE

All of us can receive emotional love in any one of the five love languages, but our primary love language is the most important. If we receive heavy doses of love in our primary language, then expressions of the other four can be sprinkled in like icing on the cake. But if we don't receive an adequate supply of our primary love language, we will not feel loved even though our spouse is sincerely speaking some of the other languages. Thus, the key to making sex an act of love is to make sure we understand and regularly speak our spouse's primary love language.

How do you discover your spouse's primary love language? Let me ask three questions. The first one is, How does your spouse most often express love to other people? If your spouse is a physical toucher, it probably means he or she receives love by physical touch. If your spouse is constantly verbally affirming people, words of affirmation is probably his or her love language. If your spouse gives gifts to others on every possible occasion, then receiving gifts may be the most important expression of love to your spouse.

A second question is, What does your spouse complain about most often? We typically get irritated when our spouse complains, but complaints reveal the need of the heart. If your husband says, "We don't spend any time together," he is telling you that quality time is his love language. When you return from a business trip, if your wife says, "You didn't bring me anything," she is telling you that receiving gifts is the most effective language to her.

A third question is, What does your spouse request of you most often? If your spouse rather regularly says, "Can we take a walk after dinner tonight?" or "Do you think we could get a weekend away within the next month?" you are being asked for quality time. If your spouse says, "Would you give me a backrub?" the request is for physical touch. If your spouse asks, "Did I do all right with that?" he or she is asking for affirming words.

The answers to these three questions will reveal your spouse's primary love language.

When you learn to speak your spouse's love language, you will see a significant difference in the emotional climate of your marriage. Remember, love's most effective language is not what *you think* would make your spouse feel loved, it is what *your spouse thinks* would make him or her feel loved. Your spouse is the expert. Don't try to impose your love language; rather, learn to speak the language that most effectively communicates love for your spouse. When you both feel loved, sex will no longer be a chore or a duty but rather a natural response. You will indeed be "making love."

PUTTING THE PRINCIPLES INTO PRACTICE

1. Do you know what your spouse's primary love language is? Do you know what yours is?

2. If you have never considered the idea of love languages before, try asking yourself the three questions suggested at the end of this chapter.

3. How might knowing your spouse's primary love language change the ways you express your love?

4. How would you like your spouse to change the way he or she expresses love to you, based on your primary love language?

6

$\mathcal{S}$he was weeping uncontrollably. "I've got to have help," she said. "I can't take it anymore. Last night, he pushed me onto the couch and gave me a thirty-minute lecture on how it was my fault that our children were not doing well in school, that if I would help them do their homework, they would make better grades. He accused me of watching television when I should be helping the children. I don't know how he could accuse me of that. He's never home in the evenings; he's always having a drink with his buddies and talking about sports. I don't get any help from him in rearing the children. He comes home at ten or eleven o'clock at night and wants to have sex.

It's unbearable! But if I refuse, he goes into a rage. So I go along with it, but I hate it." It was obvious to me that this wife and husband, though they had sex, knew nothing of making love.

As long as one spouse is inflicting pain on the other, they will never experience the satisfaction of making love. There are many arenas in which pain can be experienced. Let me share three of the most common.

EMOTIONAL PAIN

Emotional pain comes as the result of harsh language. Raised voices and condemning words are emotional bombs that explode in the human heart and destroy love.

The Hebrew Scriptures tell us, "The tongue has the power of life and death, and those who love it will eat its fruit."[1] You can kill your spouse—or you can give life—by the way you speak. When you encourage your spouse with affirming words, it creates the desire to be better. When you tear your spouse down with negative words, it creates the desire to return fire with equally damaging words.

In most marriages, emotional pain is rarely one sided. Failing to love and respect each other typically leads to condemning and berating each other. For example, the husband of the woman we met at the beginning of this chapter had this to say: "She is so critical of me, and what she says is not true. I don't hang out with the boys every night. One night a week, we enjoy Monday night football together, but the rest of the week, I'm at home working in the yard or on the house." (They were in the process of restoring an old house.) "Nothing I do is good enough for her. She blames me for all of our problems. I know I shouldn't have pushed her onto the couch, but I had had enough. When she told me it was my fault that the children were not doing well in school, I exploded. I didn't get an education. I can't help the children. She could help them, but instead, she watches television and smokes cigarettes, which I hate. The smoke is killing all of us."

Words of condemnation, like the ones this husband and wife hurled at each other, sting deeply and build more resentment. Two people who resent each other become fountains of negative words that stimulate more emotional pain. When the heart is filled with pain, there is no room left for love. The couple may withdraw from each other in order to escape the harsh words. Or, they may continue with their verbal gunfire until one of them finally capitulates. In silence they both suffer the pain of condemnation and rejection. While they may continue to have sex, they will never be able to make love until there is genuine repentance and forgiveness and until the harsh words are replaced with words of love and concern.

The good news is that if we are willing to turn from our destructive behavior and confess our own failures, not only will God forgive us, but usually our spouse will also be willing to forgive. When the walls of hurt and pain have been removed, we have the potential to learn to be lovers, to speak affirming and encouraging words that build each other up and create a desire in each other to be even better.

Some time ago, I shared the power of affirming words with a frustrated wife. She looked at me and said with all sincerity, "I hear what you are saying.

I know it would be good if I could give my husband some positive words. But to be honest with you, I can't think of anything good about him."

I paused. Finally I asked, "Does your husband ever take a shower?"

"Yes."

"How often?" I asked.

"Every day," she said.

"Then if I were you, I'd start there. Tell him, 'I appreciate your taking a shower today.' There are some men who don't."

I've never met a man about whom you couldn't find *something* good to say. I've never met a wife about whom you couldn't find *something* good to say. And when you verbalize to your spouse something you like, you have taken the first step toward learning how to make love.

PHYSICAL PAIN

Physical pain is experienced in two spheres. One is typically called physical abuse, and the other, sexual abuse. Physical abuse involves inflicting any type of bodily pain on another person. Pushing, shoving, shaking, hitting, and clawing are examples of physical abuse. Through the years, many people have sat in my office wearing long-sleeved sweaters or shirts designed to cover the bruises on their arms or with sunglasses hiding blackened eyes. Where physical abuse is a way of life, there will be no making love. The victim may acquiesce to avoid further abuse, but the heart is closed in pain.

Sexual abuse may or may not involve physical abuse such as that listed above. But even when it does not, pain is inflicted when one spouse treats the other as an object rather than a person. The husband who forces himself upon his wife sexually is abusing her. The husband who is insensitive when his wife has a painful physical condition, such as a vaginal infection, and insists on having sex anyway is also abusing her. On the other hand, the wife who refuses to get medical treatment for such conditions is abusing her husband. Such abuse stimulates pain and resentment, neither of which is conducive to making love.

Successful lovemaking requires the opposite attitude—one in which each expresses to the other, "The last thing I want to do is to hurt you, so please tell me if anything I do causes you physical pain. My desire is to give you pleasure, never to bring you pain." When this attitude is expressed both in your words and in your behavior, you will learn to make love, not just have sex.

SPIRITUAL PAIN

For the Christian, sex has a spiritual dimension. Recognizing intercourse as a gift from God and marriage as the setting in which God intended men and women to experience sex, the Christian comes to sex with a deep sense of gratitude to God. This gratitude may even be expressed in the middle of lovemaking. The pleasure between husband and wife is so intense that one's heart may be lifted in praise and thanksgiving to God for bringing them to each other.

However, this entire spiritual dimension is lost if one spouse chooses to walk away from God. If you are a believer and, for whatever reason, your spouse rejects God, you will experience great pain. You realize that the two of you will never reach your potential without the smile of God. If this is your situation, pray that God will give you the ability to love your spouse even when his or her behavior brings you great pain. God's love toward us is unconditional. Strive to follow his example and trust God to make your own walk with him a positive influence on your spouse.

Conversely, sexual lovemaking is greatly enhanced when a husband or wife takes the initiative to acknowledge God in all areas of life. When a husband chooses to join his wife in a time of Bible reading and prayer, he enhances their sexual experience. When she sees him taking initiative in reading Bible stories to the children and making sure the children understand the love of God, her respect for him is increased. Her spiritual hunger for God makes her want to be intimate with this man, who is seeking God. It is simply a fact. Those couples who walk closely with God will be much more successful than others in lovemaking.

PUTTING THE PRINCIPLES
INTO PRACTICE

1. Can you think of a time when your spouse inflicted emotional pain on you with harsh, condemning, blaming words? Can you think of a time in which you inflicted pain on your spouse by using such words? Have you taken the initiative to confess this painful behavior to your spouse and ask for forgiveness? If so, how did your spouse respond? If not, would you be willing to take such action today?

2. Can you think of a time in which you physically or sexually abused your spouse? Can you think of a time in which your spouse physically or sexually abused you? Have either of you taken initiative to deal with past failures in this area? If not, why not do it today?

3. Does your present walk with God create a climate that enhances your sexual relationship? Is there a decision you need to make or an action you need to take that will move

you closer to being a godly husband or a godly wife? Why not do it today?

4. Consider making the following statement to your spouse:

> I want you to know that it is my desire to bring you pleasure and never pain in any area of life. So if I ever hurt you, will you please tell me so that I can apologize?

Such a statement will greatly enhance your ability to make love, not just have sex.

7

LOVE FORGIVES PAST FAILURES

*W*hen your spouse made the decision to marry you, it was likely with the assumption that after the wedding you would behave the same way you did before the wedding. Unfortunately, that is probably not what happened. Once the euphoria of being "in love" evaporated, you went back to being "normal."

When normal behavior—that is, being selfish, demanding, and critical—leads couples into anger and resentment, many conclude that they made a mistake when they got married and that they are incompatible and will never be happy together.

They may give up, choose to divorce, and set about trying to find someone better. Unfortunately, some couples repeat this cycle two, three, and four times and are no happier in the fourth marriage than they were in the first.

There is a better way. The secret to a loving marriage is found not in running away but in learning to deal with our propensity for self-centeredness. Let me share with you the process of forgiving each other, accepting God's forgiveness, and creating a different future for your marriage.

THE FIRST STEP

The first step is to acknowledge to yourself and to God that in your efforts to meet your own needs, you have sometimes spoken and acted negatively toward your spouse. Your harsh words and hurtful behavior have created a wall between the two of you. As long as the wall exists, you will never reach your potential for making love. The walls must come down if you are to have the intimate, fulfilling relationship you desired when you got married.

In my thirty years as a marriage counselor, I have helped hundreds of couples tear down walls. It all begins with a simple spiritual exercise: Get alone with God. Admit to God that you have not been a perfect spouse. Then ask him to show you specifically where you have failed your spouse. As he brings your failures to mind, write them down. Once you have completed the list, confess these things to God, one by one. Thank him that Christ has paid the penalty for your sins and ask him to forgive you.

THE SECOND STEP

The second step may be more difficult. You must now confess these failures to your spouse and ask forgiveness. You might say something like this: "I've been thinking a lot about us lately. I realize that I am far from being a perfect spouse. In fact, the other night I asked God to show me where I have been failing you, and he gave me a rather long list. I have asked God to forgive me for these things, and if you've got a few minutes, I would like to share them with you and ask if you would be willing to forgive me, too."

If your spouse is willing to listen, then read the list and say, "I know these things are wrong. I feel bad that I have hurt you so deeply. I don't want to continue this kind of behavior. I want to be the spouse that you deserve. I'd like the chance to make it up to you, and I'm asking you if you can find it in your heart to forgive me."

Your spouse may not immediately respond with forgiveness, but at least you have opened the door for that possibility. We cannot erase our past failures, but we can confess them and request forgiveness.

After you've confessed your failures, your spouse may or may not offer a similar confession. But either way, the wall between you is not as thick because you have dealt with your side of it. When both of you confess past failures and choose to forgive each other, you will have the potential for making love, not just having sex.

GOD'S FORGIVENESS

The Scriptures indicate that when we confess our sins to God, he is always willing to forgive us.

"If we confess our sins, [God] is faithful and just and will forgive us our sins and purify us from all unrighteousness."[1] The moment we confess our sins to God, we experience the warm embrace of our heavenly Father. The barrier is removed, and we can now continue our fellowship with him.

As followers of Christ, we are instructed to forgive each other in the same way that God forgives us.[2] Forgiveness is not a feeling; forgiveness is a choice. We hear the confession of our spouse's failures and the request for forgiveness. Because we have been forgiven by God, we choose to forgive each other's failures.

Forgiveness does not immediately remove the pain that we have experienced, nor does forgiveness necessarily remove all the consequences of what has happened. But forgiveness does remove the barrier between us and allows us to continue our relationship.

CREATING A DIFFERENT FUTURE

Now that we have dealt with past failures, we are ready to create a different future for the two of us. If we simply go back to "doing what comes naturally," we will eventually create new walls between us. Instead of living a natural life, Christians are called to live a supernatural life. We have within us the power of the Holy Spirit to change our self-centered attitudes into attitudes of unselfish love. Instead of looking out for only our own interests, we learn to look out for the interests of our spouse.

God loves your spouse unconditionally, just as he loves you. He wants you to be his channel of expressing his love to your spouse. This is true even when your spouse is not loving you.

In describing God's love, the apostle Paul said, "God demonstrates his own love for us in this: While we were still sinners, Christ died for us."[3] He is our model. He did not love us because we loved him; he loved us when we were walking away from him. That is the kind of love we are to demonstrate to our spouse. Does that sound impossible? It is, without the help of God. But again, Paul instructs us, "God has poured out his love into our hearts by the Holy Spirit."[4] We are simply passing to our spouse the love that God has poured out in our hearts.

Therefore, the daily prayer of the Christian husband or wife should be, "Lord, fill my heart with your love so I can express it to my spouse. Bring to my mind ways in which I can express your love today." That is a prayer that God will answer. You will become a channel of love to your spouse, and in due time, your spouse will likely reciprocate.

This does not mean that you will never again lose your temper or say a harsh word or treat your spouse unkindly. It does mean that whenever this happens you will try to be quick to apologize, seek to make restitution, and ask for forgiveness. You will refuse to let the wall be erected again.

Christians are not perfect, but Christians are willing to deal with their failures and willing to forgive when there is confession and repentance. Because we have been forgiven by God, we choose to forgive each other. Practicing genuine confession and genuine forgiveness is the road to making love, not just having sex.

PUTTING THE PRINCIPLES
INTO PRACTICE

1. Do you sense that there is a wall between you and your spouse that hinders you from having the sexual intimacy you desire?

2. If so, would you be willing to ask God to show you your own failures in the marriage? As they come to your mind, write them down. Then confess your failures to God and accept his forgiveness.

3. Would you be willing to confess these failures to your spouse and ask his or her forgiveness? (You may want to read again the confession statement found on page 73.) Your spouse may or may not immediately forgive you. But your confession paves the way for the potential of forgiveness and reconciliation.

8

MAKING LOVE IS A LIFELONG JOURNEY

$\mathcal{S}$exual compatibility is not something we achieve once and for all, and then forever thereafter, sex is heavenly. All of life is in a constant process of change. Our sexual desires are affected by many variables. Disease and sickness can radically impact our sexual desires and abilities. The arrival of children often upsets the sexual equilibrium between new parents. All of us experience physical and emotional stress, with our levels of stress fluctuating from time to time. Extremely stressful periods of life can greatly impact a couple's sexual relationship. Accepting too many responsibilities at work, at church, in the community, or with extended family members can also affect their level of sexual satisfaction.

When the captain of a ship realizes that he is not on course to reach his destination, he must adjust the course. In marriage, too, we must from time to time evaluate our sexual relationship and be willing to make course corrections. If we simply drift, we will drift apart. But if we put our oars in the water, we can row our way back to mutual sexual fulfillment.

The good news is that we can do it. However, it will require communication, sensitivity, and a conscious decision to make our marriages a priority.

COMMUNICATION

Making necessary course corrections over time requires a couple's ongoing willingness to talk openly and honestly about their sexual relationship. Husbands and wives who take the approach that sex is not something to be talked about but just something to do will likely never become great lovers.

Marriage partners will always have different thoughts, ideas, desires, and emotions. If they are going to reach the destination of fulfilling, satisfying lovemaking, they must take the time for open communication.

Here are some questions I have encouraged couples to ask each other in order to communicate more effectively about their sexual relationship:

- On a scale of 1–10, how satisfied are you with our sexual relationship? (If the answer is 9 or 10, a follow-up question would be, What can we do to keep it at this level? If the answer is 8 or below, a follow-up question is, What can we do to make it better?)

- What do you wish I would do—or stop doing—to make our sexual relationship better for you?

- If I could make one change to enhance our sexual relationship, what would it be?

These questions open the door for your spouse to give you honest feedback.

SENSITIVITY

Once you begin communicating about your sexual relationship, it is not enough to simply listen to what your spouse says or to give a rebuttal. What is more important is that you are sensitive to your spouse's thoughts, desires, and feelings. For example, perhaps your spouse will say, "I wish you would not raise your voice and speak to me harshly. It kills my desire for sexual intimacy." Rather than being defensive, try to offer a sensitive reply, something like, "Tell me more about that. What does it sound like when I raise my voice? How does it make you feel?"

Often we are not aware of how our words or our behavior comes across to our spouse. The important thing is to be sensitive to the emotional responses our behavior creates.

If you are going to have an intimate sexual relationship with your spouse, it may well mean that you must change some behavior patterns learned in your family of origin. Many of us grew up in homes where loud talking was simply the norm. No one was especially offended by such talk. However, your spouse did not grow up in your family. Perhaps your spouse grew up in a soft-spoken family, and your loudness sounds harsh. A husband cannot treat his wife in the same way that his father treated his mother and expect his spouse to respond in the same manner as his mother. His wife is a totally different person, and his behavior affects her in a different way.

A wife may speak with sarcasm, or she may have negative responses to every idea her husband shares. To her, these are natural responses because this is how her mother spoke. But to him, they feel like a sword piercing his heart. They kill his motivation to communicate, and the two of them grow apart. The wife who wants to be a good lover must be sensitive to her husband's emotional responses to her behavior.

Remember, you are not locked into the patterns of speech and behavior that you learned as a child. As an adult you have the capacity, with the help of God, to change patterns that are detrimental to your marital relationship. If you want to make love and not just have sex, you must be sensitive to your spouse's perceptions and be willing to change.

MAKING MARRIAGE A PRIORITY

The couple who are truly following Christ will never be satisfied simply with having sex. They want to be lovers, and they are willing to take the time and effort necessary to make that a reality.

The bottom line is that both of you must make your marriage a priority. Only that decision will provide the motivation you need to do the hard work of communicating and being sensitive to each other. Under the lordship of Christ, you decide to have the kind of marriage that God intended for you. You realize that the sexual part of the marriage is an extremely important part of the marriage. Thus, you are motivated to talk and listen; respect each other's ideas, desires, and emotions; and work together to create God's ideal.

God never designed sex to be put on the shelf after the honeymoon or after the children arrive or after fifteen years of marriage. You are sexual creatures as long as you live, and you need to relate to each other sexually, seeking to give each other pleasure throughout a lifetime.

The couples who will make love for a lifetime are the couples who are committed to learning. They will from time to time read a book on the sexual aspect of marriage and discuss its contents and try to make things better for each other. They will periodically attend a marriage seminar and seek to discover ideas that will strengthen their relationship. If crises develop and they realize that their relationship is in danger, they will reach out for the help of a pastor or counselor. They are mature enough to realize that everyone needs help from time to time.

The mature couple will leave no stone unturned in an effort to discover God's ideal—mutual sexual fulfillment. They will never be satisfied to simply have sex. They desire to make love and to keep love alive for a lifetime.

PUTTING THE PRINCIPLES INTO PRACTICE

1. Choose one of the following questions as a means of opening communication with your spouse:

On a scale of 1–10, how satisfied are you with our sexual relationship? If the answer is 9 or 10, follow up with this question: What can we do to keep it there? If the answer is 8 or below, follow up with this question: What can we do to enhance our relationship?

What do you wish I would do—or stop doing—to make our sexual relationship better for you? You may wish to use the lists found in "What Husbands Wish" (page 97) and "What Wives Wish" (page 105) to stimulate your thinking.

If I could make one change to enhance our sexual relationship, what would it be?

2. When was the last time you attended a marriage enrichment seminar or attended a class on marriage? If it has been more than a year, why not try to schedule such an event sometime during the next year?

3. Perhaps you and your spouse would like to select one of the books on the resource page

at the end of this book to read together. The two of you can read and discuss a chapter each week with a view toward enhancing your sexual relationship. Many couples have found such an exercise extremely helpful.

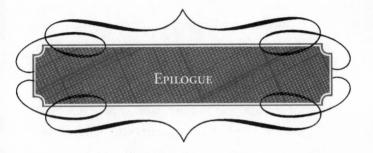

$\mathcal{T}$he challenge for many couples today is that they have had little or no training in how to love each other. They get married in the euphoria of being "in love." And they fully intend to live happily ever after. They envision sex as being heavenly and without effort. However, when they come down off the emotional high of being "in love" (the average life span of the euphoria is two years), their visions of heaven turn into nightmares of conflict. Sex becomes a battleground, and they blame each other for their unhappiness. The message of this book is that if you can learn to make love rather than just having sex, your dreams can come true and sexual union will lead both of you to the deep connection you desire.

If your sexual relationship is not what you desire it to be, don't despair. We are creatures of change, and if we make the right choices, we can change for the better. Your choices will influence the choices of your spouse, and in time, your spouse may well reciprocate. Every day our words and behavior influence our spouse in a negative way or a positive way. We determine the direction of our influence. I strongly encourage you to pray daily that God will make you a lover, not simply one who seeks to satisfy your sexual desires.

If you find this book helpful, I hope you will share it with a friend. If you have stories to share with me, I invite you to click on the Contact link at www.garychapman.org.

SOME THOUGHTS WORTH REMEMBERING

- Throughout human history, love and sex have always been related. However, in contemporary culture, love and sex have been equated.

- Christians have always viewed marriage as a sacred relationship between a husband and wife, instituted by God. The sexual union between the husband and wife is seen as a living symbol of their deep companionship.

- A husband can desire to have sexual intercourse even when things are not right in the relationship. In fact, he often thinks that having sex will solve the problems.

- On the other hand, a wife wants things to be made right before having sexual intercourse. Sex itself does not solve problems for her.

- It often requires far more energy, effort, and time for a woman to experience orgasm than it does for a man. Sometimes, because of fatigue or other distractions, a wife simply does not desire to go through the entire process.

- If a husband and wife simply do "what comes naturally," they will never learn to make love. The best that may happen is that one of them will find partial fulfillment and the other will feel used.

- Making love is about giving, not demanding. When we focus on creating an atmosphere of love in which we are genuinely seeking to affirm our spouse, we will eventually hear the invitation.

ɪᴐ Without love, the world looks bleak, and sex is at best a temporary oasis in a barren desert.

ɪᴐ The average life span of the "in love" experience is two years. We don't stay obsessed with each other forever. If we did, we would never accomplish anything.

ɪᴐ Emotional love can be restored, but it doesn't happen simply with the passing of time. It comes only when couples choose the attitude of love and find meaningful ways to express it. Loving actions stimulate loving feelings.

ɪᴐ Sexual fulfillment has little to do with technique but much to do with attitude, words, and actions.

ɪᴐ The most powerful prayer you can pray for your marriage is, "Lord, give me the

attitude of Christ toward my spouse."
Pray that prayer daily. It is a prayer that
God will answer.

- Two people who resent each other
become fountains of negative words that
stimulate more emotional pain. When the
heart is filled with pain, there is no room
left for love.

- Forgiveness is not a feeling; forgiveness is
a choice. Because we have been forgiven
by God, we choose to forgive each other's
failures.

- Forgiveness does not immediately remove
the pain that we have experienced, nor
does forgiveness necessarily remove all the
consequences of what has happened. But
forgiveness does remove the barrier
between us and allows us to continue our
relationship.

- God loves your spouse unconditionally,
just as he loves you. He wants you to be
his channel of expressing his love to your

spouse. This is true even when your
spouse is not loving you.

☞ Extremely stressful periods of life can
greatly impact a couple's sexual relationship. Accepting too many responsibilities
at work, at church, in the community, or
with extended family members can also
greatly affect their level of sexual
satisfaction.

☞ You are not locked into the patterns of
speech and behavior that you learned as a
child. As an adult you have the capacity,
with the help of God, to change patterns
that are detrimental to your marital
relationship. If you want to make love
and not just have sex, you must be
sensitive to your spouse's perceptions and
be willing to change.

*W*hat do you wish your wife would do—or stop doing—to make the sexual relationship better for you? Check ☑ the wishes you would like to share with her.

☐ I wish she would learn to enjoy sex rather than looking at it as an obligation.

☐ I wish we would communicate our sexual interests earlier in the day. If both of us are on the same page at bedtime, it can prevent disappointments and create a great time.

☐ I wish she would not talk about my weight.

☐ I wish she would wear sexy clothes and "light my fire."

☐ I wish my wife wanted to have sex more often. She is so busy.

☐ I wish she would join me in an exercise program.

☐ I wish she would watch more romantic movies with me.

☐ I wish we could spend more quality time together.

☐ I wish she would be open to oral sex.

☐ I wish my wife would initiate sex more often. It is measurably more enjoyable for me when she is more active in getting things started.

☐ I wish she would open up more and talk about this part of our marriage.

☐ I never remember when my wife's menstrual cycle is, and I don't seem to figure it out until my motor is already running. I'm asking for a subtle little reminder.

☐ I wish we had sex more often and that she wanted it as much as I do.

☐ I wish she would take more pride in her appearance. No sweat suits in bed.

☐ I wish my wife would stop acting like we have to make an appointment for sex and that she would be more spontaneous.

☐ I wish my wife would be more vocal while making love. Sound is important.

☐ I wish she would be patient and release me from my obligation when her drive for sex is stronger than mine.

☐ I wish she were open to date nights where we could just enjoy doing things together.

☐ I wish there were some variety in our

sexual relationship and that we would have sex more often.

☐ I wish she had a traffic light above her head that would tell me when she's "ready to go." I don't like it when I try to initiate sex and I am rejected.

☐ I wish my wife could have sex without so much romance to get it started.

☐ I wish our work schedules could be coordinated. Because we work on different shifts, we have very little time together, thus very little sex.

☐ I wish we had sex more than once a year. I wish her mind was on me rather than on her mom and dad. Maybe when they die, we can have sex.

☐ I wish my wife saw sex more as a mutual experience. It seems more and more about meeting my needs rather than an exciting experience for us.

☐ I wish I didn't have to use condoms every

time we have intercourse. I wish she
would take birth-control pills.

☐ I wish she would allow herself to let go
of past experiences and enjoy our sexual
relationship.

☐ I wish she would not go to bed early so
many nights. I wish we could have time
to talk and cuddle.

☐ I wish we could make love in the morn-
ings when we are both awake.

☐ I wish my wife would seek medical advice
for a physical problem she has that makes
it painful for her to have sex. I'm frustrated and don't know why she won't seek
help.

☐ I wish the word *no* would disappear from
her vocabulary.

☐ I wish she would kick the kids out of our
bedroom. I'm wondering if she is just
using them to avoid having sex.

☐ I wish that my wife would not bring up problems when we are trying to have sex. We can discuss problems at another time.

☐ Over the years her lingerie closet has become fuller but is opened less often. She is a beautiful woman, and I would enjoy seeing her open that closet more often.

☐ I wish she would not have projects every night that keep us busy but apart.

☐ I wish she would stay awake when we are making love. Her pleasure is just as important as mine, and it's not fun for me when I am making love with a corpse.

☐ I wish we could dedicate more time to our physical relationship. I wish she understood the importance of it. I miss the closeness.

☐ I wish she were more open to experimentation with new ideas, would let me know what she wants, and would listen to my desires. I don't want to force anything on her.

☐ I wish she would stop chitchatting during sex and just relax and enjoy it.

☐ I wish she would not expect so much of me in the way of romantic ideas. I'm willing and I try, but it never seems to be enough.

☐ I wish she would stop telling me that I don't act like I'm attracted to her. I *am* attracted to her. I don't know what else to do.

☐ I wish my wife would allow me to pleasure her sexually. She has a general attitude that sex is "nasty." I know she was sexually abused as a child, but she refuses to go for counseling.

☐ I wish she were more comfortable with her body so we could leave the lights on when we make love. I enjoy seeing her body.

☐ I wish she would make suggestions to me
   about what makes the sexual experience
   more pleasurable for her.

$\mathcal{W}$hat do you wish your husband would do—or
stop doing—to make the sexual relationship better
for you? Check ☑ the wishes you would like to
share with him.

☐ I wish he would work with me a little
more to find out what feels good for me.

☐ I wish he would take better care of his
body so that I would be more physically
attracted to him.

☐ I wish that he would stop coming on to

me constantly so I could make the first move once in a while.

☐ I wish he would not rush into lovemaking —more foreplay.

☐ I wish he would make sex spontaneous rather than ask for it and would hold me more.

☐ I wish he would stop waiting for me to initiate sex.

☐ I wish my husband would spend more time talking and cuddling instead of just jumping right in.

☐ I wish he would realize that things he does throughout the day affect sex that night.

☐ I wish I had more say about when the sexual experience would end; often he stops too soon.

☐ I wish he would spend time listening to me without the computer, radio, or television competing for his attention.

☐ I wish he would listen to me and not criticize my thoughts and feelings.

☐ I wish we could have more family time together. If I feel connected, sex is better.

☐ I wish he would come to bed earlier— turn off the TV sooner, and just come snuggle (pre-sex), making "intimacy" a priority.

☐ I wish he would not come to bed thirty minutes after I've gone to sleep and start "pawing" at me.

☐ I wish he would touch me sometimes when he *doesn't* want sex. Throw a few hugs and kisses into the mix and I would feel more interested in sex.

☐ I wish he would let me know that he is proud of me and glad I am his wife.

☐ With a new baby, I am tired much of the time. I wish sex wasn't "expected" so often.

☐ I wish my husband would romance me again, with a flower, note, card, or small gift that says, "I love you."

☐ I wish he would sit on the couch with me, hold hands, and kiss rather than sleep in the recliner.

☐ I wish he would show more love to me before and after sex, so it's not just physical but also spiritual and emotional.

☐ I wish we had consistent date nights without discussing cost—just trying new things together.

☐ I wish my husband would stop treating sex like it doesn't mean anything but a "fix," stop asking all the time, and stop making me feel guilty when I'm not in the mood.

☐ I wish he would allow me to get into bed, touch him, or cuddle up next to him, even kiss him good night, and not have it always turn into sex.

☐ I wish he would realize that the way he acts when he comes home from work (grouchy, impatient, irritable) sets the tone for the night, and I don't have a switch that turns all that off and suddenly makes me want to have sex with him.

☐ I wish he would be okay with the fact that sex is not as enjoyable for me as it is for him. I actually love good massages without sex.

☐ I wish he would spend more time before sexual intimacy reaffirming how special I am—things like placing his arm around me, saying something nice about me, treating me in a way that makes me feel loved. Having been sexually abused as a child, I sometimes feel that when these things do not happen, he is just using me for my body.

☐ I wish my husband would remember that because I am post-menopausal, intercourse is painful for me. I want to please him because I love him very much.

☐ I wish he would arrange for a special night or weekend where it is just us so we could concentrate on sexual intimacy.

☐ I wish he would understand that my lack of interest has nothing to do with him. It has everything to do with my lack of time and energy and my stress level.

☐ I wish he would stop grabbing me in intimate places when I'm trying to cook dinner or accomplish a task.

☐ I wish my husband would continue to stimulate me throughout the sexual encounter instead of just at the beginning.

☐ I wish we had sex more often and that he was not so tired all the time.

☐ I wish he would not ask for sex when I'm not feeling well. I am pregnant and have morning sickness and just don't need to be shaken up like a soda bottle.

☐ I wish he would not tease or make "cat calls" when I undress.

☐ I wish he would work with me on our spiritual relationship.

☐ I wish my husband would seek help for impotency. It has been an issue for years.

☐ I wish we would plan intimate nights so we could both "get ready" for a fun evening. Sometimes spontaneous sexual encounters are exciting, but anticipation is fun, too.

☐ I wish he would stop playing solitaire on the computer instead of coming to bed.

☐ I wish he would feel more free to let me know what I am doing—right or wrong—in making the sexual experience good for him.

☐ I wish that my husband would compliment my physical appearance more often, but I want him to mean it.

☐ I wish he would talk about loving me as a person instead of talking about wanting and desiring sex. I want to feel desirable as a woman, not as someone to meet his needs.

☐ I wish he would believe that when I say, "I'm too tired," I really am too tired.

Kevin Leman, *Sheet Music: Uncovering the Secrets of Sexual Intimacy in Marriage* (Tyndale House, 2003)

Get ready to make beautiful music together! Dr. Kevin Leman's practical guide will help any couple stay "in tune" for an active, God-designed sex life. He addresses a wide spectrum of individuals—with positive, negative, or no experience—and his frank descriptions, line drawings, and warm and friendly tone will help couples find greater harmony through intimacy.

Clifford and Joyce Penner, *The Gift of Sex: A Guide to Sexual Fulfillment* (Thomas Nelson, 2003)

Internationally recognized sexual therapists Clifford and Joyce Penner draw from their vast clinical experience to help couples explore the deep, powerful, and mysterious aspects of their sexuality. Hopeful, encouraging, and highly practical, this newly revised and updated best seller is a valuable resource for any couple interested in enhancing their sexual relationship, whether newly wed or married for years.

Douglas E. Rosenau, *A Celebration of Sex: A Guide to Enjoying God's Gift of Sexual Fulfillment* (Thomas Nelson, 2002)

Dr. Douglas Rosenau is a licensed psychologist and Christian sex therapist who has for the past seventeen years used his training in theology and counseling to help Christian couples enrich and reclaim God's wonderful gift of sexuality within marriage. *A Celebration of Sex* answers specific, often unasked questions about sexual topics and presents married couples with detailed techniques and behavioral skills for deepening sexual pleasure and intimate companionship.

Ed and Gaye Wheat, *Intended for Pleasure: Sex Technique and Sexual Fulfillment in Christian Marriage* (Revell, 1997)

This is the classic manual on sex in Christian marriage, now updated and expanded. A skillful combination of biblical teaching on love and marriage, with the latest medical information on sex and sexuality. The material is presented in wholesome terms that would be of help to any married or soon-to-be-married couple.

Notes

INTRODUCTION

1. Linda J. Waite and Maggie Gallagher, *The Case for Marriage* (New York: Doubleday, 2000), 79.

CHAPTER 1

1. Genesis 2:18-25.
2. Genesis 1:28.
3. Waite and Gallagher, 124–140.
4. Song of Solomon 4:9-11, 15-16.
5. Song of Solomon 5:10-16.

CHAPTER 2

1. Deuteronomy 24:5 (NLT).
2. Kevin Leman, *Sheet Music: Uncovering the Secrets of Sexual Intimacy in Marriage* (Wheaton: Tyndale House, 2003), 103.
3. Ibid.

CHAPTER 3

1. See Ephesians 5:25.
2. 1 John 4:19 (NKJV).
3. Song of Solomon 4:1-7.
4. Song of Solomon 4:16.
5. Song of Solomon 5:1.

CHAPTER 5
1. Gary Chapman, *The Five Love Languages: How to Express Heartfelt Commitment to Your Mate* (Chicago: Northfield Publishing, 1992, 1995).
2. 1 Corinthians 8:1 (NKJV).

CHAPTER 6
1. Proverbs 18:21.

CHAPTER 7
1. 1 John 1:9.
2. See Ephesians 4:32.
3. Romans 5:8.
4. Romans 5:5.

About the Author

Dr. Gary Chapman is the author of the perennial best seller *The Five Love Languages* (more than four million copies sold) and numerous other marriage and family books. He is currently working with best-selling author Catherine Palmer on a new fiction series based on *The Four Seasons of Marriage.* Dr. Chapman is the director of Marriage and Family Life Consultants, Inc.; an internationally known speaker; and the host of *A Love Language Minute,* a syndicated radio program heard on more than one hundred stations across North America. He and his wife, Karolyn, live in North Carolina.

DO YOU KNOW WHICH SEASON
YOUR MARRIAGE IS IN?

Every marriage goes through different seasons—
the satisfaction and security of summer, the
hopefulness and anticipation of spring, the
change and uncertainty of fall, and the icy
bitterness of winter. Find out which season your
marriage is currently in and learn the strategies
that will strengthen your relationship through
every season of marriage.

Available now in stores and online!

Take the free marriage-satisfaction quiz at
www.4seasonsofmarriage.com

CP0087

Introducing the

CHAPMAN GUIDES

Simple solutions to life's most difficult problems

EVERYBODY WINS

*The Chapman Guide to
Solving Conflicts Without Arguing*

CONFLICT IS INEVITABLE.
ARGUING IS A CHOICE.

Relationship expert Dr. Gary Chapman provides a simple
blueprint to help you and your spouse find win-win
solutions to everyday disagreements and leave both of you
feeling loved, listened to, and appreciated.

HOME IMPROVEMENTS

*The Chapman Guide to
Negotiating Change With Your Spouse*

IS YOUR SPOUSE'S BEHAVIOR
DRIVING YOU CRAZY?

Over time, annoying little habits can wreak havoc on a
relationship. After years of counseling battle-weary couples,
Dr. Gary Chapman has developed a simple and effective
approach that will help you and your spouse turn those
irritating behaviors around once and for all.

Profit Sharing

The Chapman Guide to
Making Money an Asset in Your Marriage

WHEN YOURS AND MINE BECOME OURS.

Money is often listed as the number-one source of conflict in marriage. In this simple and practical guide, Dr. Gary Chapman shows couples how to work together as a team to manage their finances.

Now What?

The Chapman Guide to
Marriage After Children

AND THEN THERE WERE THREE.

In his trademark simple, direct, conversational style, relationship expert Dr. Gary Chapman answers the age-old question, "How do we keep our marriage alive now that the children have arrived?"

Available now in stores and online!

CP0072

From the *New York Times* best-selling author

GARY CHAPMAN
—— and CBA best-selling author ——
CATHERINE PALMER

comes a new fiction series based on Dr. Chapman's
nonfiction book *The Four Seasons of Marriage*.

Better marriages are always in season!

Meet four couples who live, work,

and dream in Deepwater Cove.

You'll encounter quirky neighbors,

see struggles you've faced, and come

to realize that—even when it comes

to marriage—winter won't

last forever!

TYNDALE
FICTION

Visit **www.fourseasonsofmarriage.com**
for more information.

CP0019